Making a Difference OUTSIDE

by
Hermione Redshaw

Minneapolis, Minnesota

Credits: All images courtesy of Shutterstock.com. With thanks to Getty Images, Thinkstock Photo, and iStockphoto. Recurring images © Weshitelist (font), AnastasiaNi (background pattern), GoodStudio (vectors). Cover © Oleh Svetiukha, GoodStudio. 2&3 © Oleh Svetiukha. 4&5 © Sunny studio, Ulza. 6&7 © Gregory Johnston, FluidMediaFactory. 8&9 © Lana Sham, Dernkadel, proxyminde, Nataliia Suietska, Siam Stock. 10&11 © Rvector, Magura, JMichl, Wasuta23. 12&13 © Leoniek van der Vliet, moj0j0, Patrick Foto, StockSmartStart. 14&15 © nada54, Monkey Business Images. 16&17 © vectortatu, Waridsara_HappyChildren, Ermolaev Alexander. 18&19 © encierro, Julia Moiseenko, A3pfamily, Lolostock. 20&21 © Natee K Jindakum, Tatevosian Yana. 22&23 © Igoror, Villiers Steyn, JasminkaM, VectorSun58, Orakunya.

Library of Congress Cataloging-in-Publication Data is available at www.loc.gov or upon request from the publisher.

ISBN: 979-8-88509-361-3 (hardcover)
ISBN: 979-8-88509-483-2 (paperback)
ISBN: 979-8-88509-598-3 (ebook)

© 2023 Booklife Publishing
This edition is published by arrangement with Booklife Publishing.

North American adaptations © 2023 Bearport Publishing Company. All rights reserved. No part of this publication may be reproduced in whole or in part, stored in any retrieval system, or transmitted in any form or by any means, electronic, mechanical, photocopying, recording, or otherwise, without written permission from the publisher.

For more information, write to Bearport Publishing, 5357 Penn Avenue South, Minneapolis, MN 55419.

CONTENTS

The Great Outdoors............ 4
Lots of Life Outside 6
Keeping Creatures Comfy 8
Pets Outside 10
Don't Squash Me! 12
Stick to the Paths............. 14
Keep Our Planet Clean 16
Plant a Tree 18
Grow Your Own Vegetables 20
The Compost Bucket 22
Glossary 24
Index 24

THE GREAT OUTDOORS

We share Earth with many plants and animals. Our **planet** is home to all of us, so we must take care of it.

There's a lot you can do to help the things that live in nature. You can make a difference. Let's go save the world outside!

LOTS OF LIFE OUTSIDE

You can probably find different plants and animals outside where you live. There may be bugs under a rock or squirrels climbing a tree.

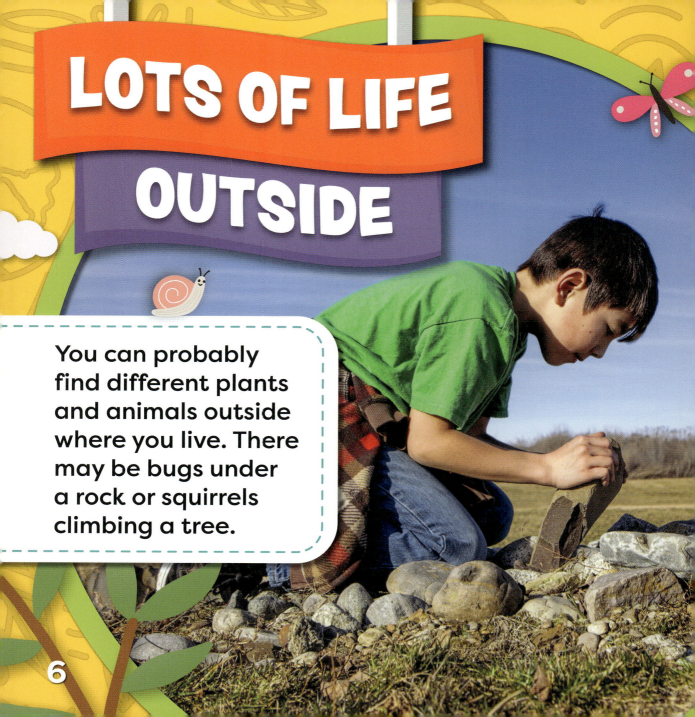

All these living things need each other. If some kinds of animals or plants can no longer live in an area, it changes life for other things there, too. That's why it is important for us to take care of outdoor areas.

KEEPING CREATURES COMFY

Different creatures make their homes with different things. We must care for them all. Can you spot any of these near where you live?

Wood makes a good home for many kinds of bugs. Some bugs even eat wood.

Flowers provide food for bees. When bees eat from many flowers, it helps the plants grow.

Ponds help feed the plants and animals near them. They are a good **habitat** for fish and frogs.

PETS OUTSIDE

Some pets can be scary to small creatures in nature. Try to stop your dog from chasing animals. If you take your dog on a walk, use a leash.

Keep an eye on pet cats when they are outside. Cats sometimes eat birds or other creatures. Putting a bell on your cat's collar can help warn these animals when your pet is coming.

DON'T SQUASH ME!

Every creature is important to our planet. That's why you shouldn't squash insects in nature, even if they scare you.

Sometimes, bugs make their way inside. If that happens, don't panic! Carefully catch them and set them free outside.

You can use an upside-down glass with a piece of paper underneath to move bugs safely.

STICK TO THE PATHS

If you go hiking, stay on the paths. Making your own way through grass and plants could harm a small creature's home or food.

Staying on the paths will protect you, too. Some plants and animals can be harmful to humans.

You don't want to get stung by these stinging nettles!

KEEP OUR PLANET CLEAN

Leaving trash on the ground is harmful to animals. If they eat it, they can get sick. Always be sure to clean up after yourself when you are outside.

Pick up litter, even if it's not your own. Make sure it ends up in a trash can or **recycling** bin. If you can't find one nearby, you can take the litter home to throw away.

Things made of paper, plastic, glass, or metal can be recycled.

PLANT A TREE

Trees let out **oxygen**, which is something all living things need to breathe. But many trees are chopped down to make paper or to clear land for buildings.

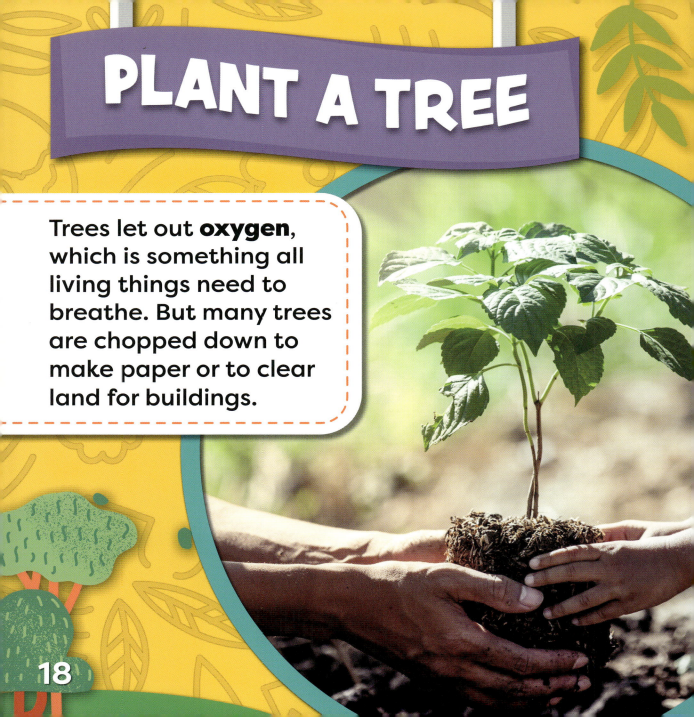

Thankfully, you can help by planting a tree! Here are a few steps to care for your tree.

Leave a small dip in the soil closest to the tree trunk so water can collect there.

If your tree is leaning or falling over, tie a stake to it.

Wrap something around your tree to protect it.

19

GROW YOUR OWN VEGETABLES

Planting a vegetable garden can help Earth, too. The veggies in grocery stores come from big farms. Often, they travel a long way in trucks and boats.

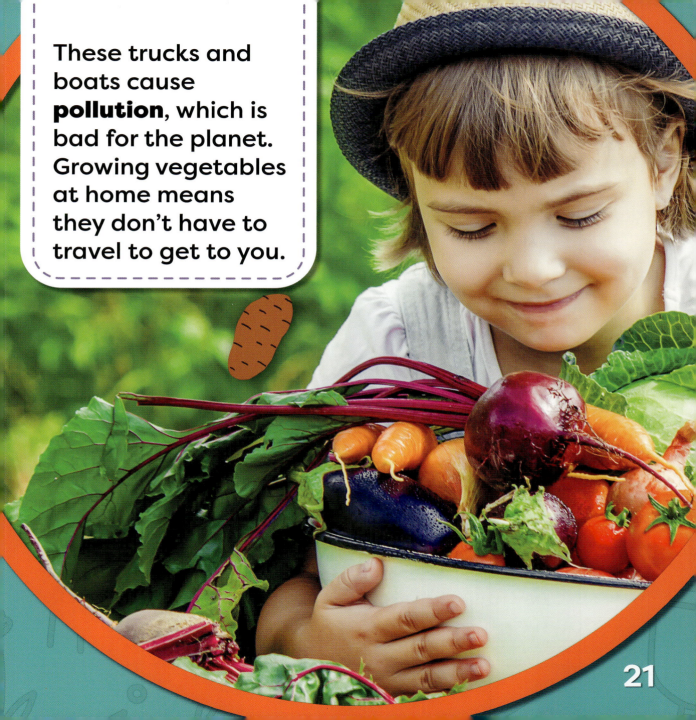

These trucks and boats cause **pollution**, which is bad for the planet. Growing vegetables at home means they don't have to travel to get to you.

THE COMPOST BUCKET

Composting is a great way to reduce waste and help your garden grow. How does it work? Food scraps go in a special bucket. There, they break down and become dirt for growing plants.

Here's how to start a compost bucket.

1. Add soil to a bucket with air holes.
2. After meals, put any food scraps into the bucket.
3. Stir the food with the soil and add a little water.
4. The food will slowly break down in the soil. Then, you can use it to grow more food!

GLOSSARY

composting gathering food scraps so it can be used in soil to help plants grow

habitat a place in nature where an animal lives

oxygen something in the air that living things need in order to survive

planet a large, round object that circles the sun

pollution harmful things being added to nature

recycling turning used, unwanted things into new, useful things

INDEX

animals 4, 6–16
compost 22–23
garden 20, 22
litter 17
paths 14–15
pollution 21
recycling 17
trees 6, 18–19
vegetables 20–21